Presented to:

_____

By:

_____

Date:

_____

Bless This
HOME

CREATING A PLACE OF LOVE & WARMTH

HONOR **HB** BOOKS

FROM DAVID C. COOK

BLESS THIS HOME
Published by Honor Books®, an imprint of
David C. Cook
4050 Lee Vance View
Colorado Springs, CO 80918 U.S.A.

David C. Cook Distribution Canada
55 Woodslee Avenue, Paris, Ontario, Canada N3L 3E5

David C. Cook U.K., Kingsway Communications
Eastbourne, East Sussex BN23 6NT, England

David C. Cook and the graphic circle C logo
are registered trademarks of Cook Communications Ministries.

The Web site addresses recommended throughout this book are offered as a resource to
you. These Web sites are not intended in any way to be or imply an endorsement on the
part of Cook Communications Ministries, nor do we vouch for their content.

ISBN 978-1-56292-952-7

© 2007 by Honor Books
Manuscript written and compiled by Shanna D. Gregor

Cover Design: The DesignWorks Group
Cover Photo: © Photodisc/Getty Images

Printed in Canada
First Edition 2007

1 2 3 4 5 6 7 8 9 10
061407

CONTENTS

INTRODUCTION

Bless This Home is a celebration of the harmony we find when the house becomes a home. Family gathered around the table, a fire crackling on the hearth, a neighbor's smile and wave … so many blessings flow from that special place we call home. It's where we recharge our batteries, host our friends and neighbors, and nurture our family.

As you snuggle up with this encouraging book sure to warm your heart, you'll discover *Bless This Home* is the perfect way to say, "Welcome Home."

Making My House a
HOME

*By wisdom a house is built, and
through understanding it is established;
through knowledge its rooms are filled
with rare and beautiful treasures.*

PROVERBS 24:3-4

WHAT MAKES A HOUSE A HOME?

Hang artwork and family pictures on the walls.

Mark the doorframe as the children grow tall.

Light a candle, or two.

Fill the house with family for the holidays.

Gather friends for a meal.

Live all four seasons under its roof.

Laugh together.

Cry together.

Celebrate good news.

Mourn a loss.

Close the door to a final good-bye.

Open your hearts to a wonderful welcome.

Play together, pray together.

When a place leaves
amazingly warm and precious
memories in your heart,
then it is home.

A home overflowing with heart is a living thing.
It promises growth, blessing, and stability to all who live
    there.
It is a place of warmth when the world turns cold.
It extends a handful of hope to replace disappointment.
It fills our souls with nourishment when we are
    hungry for encouragement and love.

For in the day of trouble he will keep me safe in
his dwelling; he will hide me in the shelter of his
tabernacle and set me high upon a rock.

PSALM 27:5

The pleasure of leaving home, care free, with no concern
but to enjoy, has also as a pendant the pleasure of
coming back to the old hearthstone, the home to
which, however traveled, the heart still fondly
turns, ignoring the burden of its anxieties and cares.

—Herman Melville

Memories of Home

There is something warm and inviting about *going home*. For most of us thoughts of home immediately invoke images of a place of safety and protection, feelings of love and acceptance, and a sense of belonging.

The aroma of freshly baked chocolate chip cookies or crisp autumn air can push the play button of our childhood memories: memories of less responsibility and more laughter allow us to strengthen ourselves for the challenges we face.

We want to give our own families a home filled with memories that they'll cherish like the ones that warm your heart and refresh your soul today as you recall your childhood home. In all that we gain as we grow older, we hold tight to our memories of what made our house a home.

A house is a home when it shelters
the body and comforts the soul.

—Phillip Moffit

———————

The home should be the treasure chest of living.

—Le Corbusier

———————

For where your treasure is, there
will your heart be also.

MATTHEW 6:21 AB

———————

You called me, and I came home to your heart.

—Robert Browning

GOD'S BLESSINGS COMING AND GOING

All these blessings will come down on you and
spread out beyond you because you have
responded to the Voice of GOD, your God:
GOD's blessing inside the city,
GOD's blessing in the country;
GOD's blessing on your children,
the crops of your land,
the young of your livestock,
the calves of your herds,
the lambs of your flocks.
GOD's blessing on your basket and bread bowl;
GOD's blessing in your coming in,
GOD's blessing in your going out.

DEUTERONOMY 28:2–6 MSG

---

*Home is the place you'll find
someone to hold you tight, where
someone is always there to kiss
you good night.*

Blessing for a New Home

May this new home be more than just a physical house, but rather may it be a home filled with life and love. May it be filled with laughter and good cheer, and may it be a place where good memories are made.

May there be harmony among those who dwell here, and may strife be turned out of doors. May each member of the family honor one another, and may all be treated with respect. May only kind words be spoken here and harsh words never uttered. May it be a place of growth and grace, a happy dwelling place.

May light fill every chamber, and may those who live here be a beacon of hope to draw those who are weary and burdened. May every person who crosses the threshold be met with your peace and find a safe harbor, a place of refuge. May they leave better than when they arrived, refreshed and restored.

Amen.

Home—that blessed word, which opens to the human heart the most perfect glimpse of heaven, and helps to carry it thither, as on an angel's wings.

—Lydia M. Child

———————

How lovely is your dwelling place,
O LORD Almighty!
My soul yearns, even faints, for the courts
of the LORD; my heart and my flesh cry
out for the living God.
Even the sparrow has found a home, and the
swallow a nest for herself, where she may have
her young—a place near your altar, O LORD
Almighty, my King and my God.
Blessed are those who dwell in your house; they
are ever praising you.

PSALM 84:1–4

Making the White House a Home

W aiting for the birth of her son, Jacqueline Kennedy pondered her pending role as First Lady of the United States. "The first obligation," she told a friend, must be "taking care of the President." Her children would be her next responsibility: "I don't want them to be brought up by nurses and Secret Service men. I will make every effort to be with my children even more now."

Jacqueline Kennedy's social secretary, Tish Baldrige, described a few of the First Lady's plans to make 1600 Pennsylvania Avenue a home when she said, "One of the rooms will become—for the first time since 1901—a nursery."[1]

A man travels the world over in search of what he needs and returns home to find it.

—George Moore

Keep the home fires burning,
While your hearts are yearning,
Though your lads are far away
They dream of home.
There's a silver lining
Through the dark cloud shining;
Turn the dark cloud inside out,
Till the boys come home.[2]

—Lena Guilbert Ford

[The lost son] returned home to his father. And while he was still a long distance away, his father saw him coming. Filled with love and compassion, he ran to his son, embraced him, and kissed him.

LUKE 15:20 NLT

The little smiling cottage! where at eve
He meets his rosy children at the door,
Prattling their welcomes, and his honest wife,
With good brown cake and bacon slice, intent
To cheer his hunger after labor hard.

—Sir Edward Dyer

A house is made of walls and beams; a home is
built with love and dreams.

—Author Unknown

---

*A house with people coming and
going always looks like its smiling
at you from across the street.*

PRAYER FOR THE HOME

Peace, unto this house, I pray,
Keep terror and despair away;
Shield it from evil and let sin
Never find lodging room within.
May never in these walls be heard
The hateful or accusing word.
Grant that its warm and mellow light
May be to all a beacon bright,
A flaming symbol that shall stir
The beating pulse of him or her
Who finds this door and seems to say,
"Here end the trials of the day.

Hold us together, gentle Lord,
Who sit about this humble board;
May we be spared the cruel fate
Of those whom hatreds separate;
Here let love bind us fast, that we
May know the joys of unity.
Lord, this humble house we'd keep
Sweet with play and calm with sleep.
Help us so that we may give
Beauty to the lives we live.
Let Thy love and let Thy grace
Shine upon our dwelling place.[3]

—Edgar Guest

*If ever household affections and loves are grace-
ful things, they are graceful in the poor. The ties
that bind the wealthy and the proud to home
may be forged on earth, but those which link the
poor man to his humble hearth are of the true
metal and bear the stamp of heaven.*

—Charles Dickens

Home and heaven are not so far separated as we
sometimes think. Nay, they are not separated at
all, for they are both in the same great building.
Home is the lower story, and is located down
here on the ground floor; heaven is above stairs,
in the second and third stories; and, as one after
another the family is called to come up higher,
that which seemed to be such a strange place
begins to wear a familiar aspect; and, when at
last not one is left below, the home is transferred
to heaven, and heaven is home.

—Alexander Dickson

A hundred years from now, it will not matter what my bank account was, the sort of house I lived in, or the make of car I drove. But the world may be different, because I was important in the life of a child.

—Author Unknown

If the shelves are dusty and the pots don't shine, it's because I have better things to do with my time.

—Author Unknown

Good moms have sticky floors, dirty ovens, and happy kids.

—Author Unknown

A healthy family is sacred territory.

—Billy Graham

Excuse the House Called Home

Tammy walked back into the bathroom that her six- and nine-year-old boys shared to put fresh towels in the bathroom she'd just cleaned. Her heart sank when she saw the evidence that the boys had come in and washed their hands. Puddles of muddy water were still dripping down the counter and across the freshly cleaned sink and floor. She wiped the mess with the fresh towels and turned back toward the laundry room.

Her husband, Kirk, saw the look on her face and tried to console her. "Honey, we have to live here. But you know, we could buy a duplex. We could live in one side and keep the other side presentable for guests," he joked.

Tammy laughed, reaching up to hug her husband. "I guess I'm learning to let go of the task and embrace something more important—time with my family."

Cleaning your house while your kids are still growing
is like shoveling the walk before it stops snowing.

—Phyllis Diller

THANK GOD FOR DIRTY DISHES

Thank God for dirty dishes,

They have a tale to tell.

While others are going hungry,

We're eating very well.

With home and health and happiness,

I shouldn't want to fuss.

For by this stack of evidence,

God's very good to us.

—Author Unknown

The home is the bottom line of life, the anvil upon which attitudes and convictions are hammered out. [It is] ... the single most influential force in our earthly existence. No price tag can adequately reflect its value. No gauge can measure its ultimate influence ... for good or ill. It is at home, among family members, that we come to terms with circumstances. It is here life makes up its mind.

—Charles Swindoll

————————

Home is wherever you are happiest!

AUTHOR UNKNOWN

————————

Home is the wallpaper above the bed,
the family dinner table, the church bells in the
morning, the bruised shins of the playground,
the small fears that come with dusk,
the streets and squares and monuments and
shops that constitute one's first universe.[4]

—Henry Anatole Grunwald

As a mother stepped back to admire the work she'd done in her daughter's bedroom with new paint, furniture, and bedding, her teen asked, "Mom, what was your room like when you were a kid?"

The mother was quiet for a moment as she mentally journeyed decades backward in time. Then she looked at her daughter and said, "The bedroom I liked the most was really the ugliest bedroom I ever had. It was on the second story of an old stone house on a 120-acre farm. I could sit at the window and see for miles—trees, cows out in the pasture, our grain silo, all four ponds, our vegetable garden, and beautiful rolling hills that touched the sky. I imagined that in some ways that was what heaven looked like."

Home is the one place in all this world where hearts are sure of each other. It is the place of confidence. It is the place where we tear off that mask of guarded and suspicious coldness which the world forces us to wear in self-defense, and where we pour out the unreserved communications of full and confiding hearts. It is the spot where expressions of tenderness gush out without any sensation of awkwardness and without any dread of ridicule.

—Frederick W. Robertson

*Hearts and homes are
warmed by love.*

An inviting home is one that you and your family will love coming home to, and one that family and friends will feel welcome in.

———————

Home is a place you grow up wanting to leave, and grow old wanting to get back to.

—John Ed Pearce

———————

The house of the righteous stands firm.

PROVERBS 12:7

HOME AND LOVE

Just Home and Love! the words are small
Four little letters unto each;
And yet you will not find in all
The wide and gracious range of speech
Two more so tenderly complete:
When angels talk in heaven above,
I'm sure they have no words more sweet
Than Home and Love.

Just Home and Love! it's hard to guess
Which of the two were best to gain;
Home without Love is bitterness;
Love without Home is often pain.
No! each alone will seldom do;
Somehow they travel hand and glove:
If you win one you must have two,
Both Home and Love.

And if you've both, well then I'm sure

You ought to sing the whole day long;

It doesn't matter if you're poor

With these to make divine your song.

And so I praisefully repeat,

When angels talk in heaven above,

There are no words more simply sweet

Than Home and Love.

—Robert William Service

For I have chosen him, so that he may command his children and his household after him to keep the way of the LORD by doing righteousness and justice; so that the LORD may bring upon Abraham what He has spoken about him.

GENESIS 18:19 NASB

———————

A father's sermons are no greater than the lives his children live.

—Author Unknown

MY HOUSE

Here are the windows,
Here is the door.
Come on in, I'll show you more.
Here is the kitchen, the living room, too.
A bathroom, three bedrooms, and a room for you!
An attic, a chimney, and a roof above.
And my house is a home
'Cause it's filled with love!

MUSIC IN OUR HOME

Mother plays the violin.
Daddy plays the flute.
Big brother blows the horn,
toot-toot-toot-toot.
Little sister keeps the beat
By clanging on a pot.
And I try to sing along
Whether I know the words or not.

A good man leaves an inheritance
to his children's children.

A man stands tallest on his knees before his
child asking his child's forgiveness.

—Author Unknown

The wisest parents are willing to admit mistakes.

—Author Unknown

The greatest home is one filled
with hearts willing to forgive.

—Author Unknown

Home—where the porch light is always on until you find your way back into the hearts of those you love.

———————

For we know that if the tent, which is our earthly home, is destroyed (dissolved), we have from God a building, a house not made with hands, eternal in the heavens.

2 CORINTHIANS 5:1 AB

———————

In my Father's House are many mansions. I hope mine is next to yours.

The Blessing of
FAMILY

He [Cornelius] and all his family were devout and
God-fearing; he gave generously to those in
need and prayed to God regularly.

ACTS 10:2

IMAGES OF A FATHER

As we grow, we develop very personal images of what a father's character, nature, and personality look like based on our family experiences. When we don't have a positive role model in our own father, we have to work hard to learn how a good father really treats his children. The greatest gift a father can give his family is a lifestyle built on the foundation of God's Word. His children will be free to live and love God with minimal baggage to overcome.

I kneel before the Father, from whom his whole family in heaven and on earth derives its name.

EPHESIANS 3:14-15

Jesus, the only bridge that can reconcile his family to God.

Loving relationships are family's best protection against the challenges of the world.

—Bernie Wiebe

The family is the most basic unit of government. As the first community to which a person is attached and the first authority under which a person learns to live, the family establishes society's most basic values.

—Charles Colson

Marriage has in it less of beauty, but more of safety, than the single life; it has more care, but less danger; it is more merry, and more sad; it is fuller of sorrows, and fuller of joys; it lies under more burdens, but it is supported by all the strengths of love, and charity, and those burdens are delightful.

—Jeremy Taylor

As a father has compassion on his children, so the Lord has compassion on those who fear him.

PSALM 103:13

A BLESSING FOR A HUSBAND FROM HIS WIFE

I thank God for bringing you into my life. May he richly bless you and cause you to fulfill your destiny. May you grow in wisdom and understanding, so that in all situations you know the right thing to do.

May your mind be filled with creative ideas, making the world a better place because you are in it. May all your efforts be crowned with success, and may you receive promotion and financial reward as you diligently pursue your career.

May God give you strength to overcome adversity. May you be healthy and live a long life. May you be kept from temptation and protected from your enemies. May you be delivered from all harm.

May our relationship be all God means for it to be. May you understand servant leadership as you direct our household, and may we flow together as one. May we be sensitive to each other's needs, always putting the other first, and may we encourage one another, always building each other up.

May our companionship be rich and our love like the finest of wines, growing better with each passing year. May our marriage be a bit of heaven on earth.

Amen.

*God's rarest blessing is,
after all, a good woman.*

Your marriage is more than a sacred covenant
with another person. It is a spiritual discipline
designed to help you know God better, trust him
more fully, and love him more deeply.

—Gary Thomas, **Sacred Marriage**

---

*Enjoy life with the woman whom you love all the
days of your fleeting life which He has given to
you under the sun; for this is your reward in life.*

ECCLESIASTES 9:9 NASB

---

*The man who finds a wife finds a good thing;
she is a blessing to him from the Lord.*

PROVERBS 18:22 TLB

A BLESSING FOR A WIFE
FROM HER HUSBAND

May you be blessed for being such a blessing to me. May you be empowered to fulfill God's plan for your life, and may he fill you with his wisdom as you approach each role that you fill.

May you know how much I admire you and appreciate what you bring to our marriage. May I be the husband you need me to be, and may our relationship satisfy your needs for romance and intimacy.

May your role as a mother be filled with joy as you watch our children grow up. As they take their place in the world, may you witness abundant fruit from your faithful nurturing and training.

May you be blessed with friends, both old and new, and may you enrich one another in those relationships. May you experience success in your career, and may you have opportunities to exercise your areas of expertise. May you receive promotion as you continue to grow in the special gifts God has given the world through you.

May peace surround you to shield you from anxiety and stress. May you be filled with joy and receive the desires of your heart.

Amen.

Love puts the fun in together,
The sad in apart,
The hope in tomorrow,
The joy in the heart.

———————

He was my cream, and I was his coffee. And when you poured us together, it was something.

—Josephine Baker

———————

A happy marriage is the union of two good forgivers.

—Elbert Green Hubbard

God sets the lonely in families.

PSALM 68:6

---

*A happy family is but
an earlier heaven.*

A PRAYER FOR THE FAMILY

May God who gives patience, steadiness, and encouragement help you to live in complete harmony with each other—each with the attitude of Christ toward the other.

ROMANS 15:5 TLB

Boy

Function: *noun*

Meaning: *a noise with dirt on it*

—Not Your Average Dictionary

First a bother,
Then a brother,
Now a friend.

He settles the barren woman in her home as a
happy mother of children.

PSALM 113:9

The most beautiful sound in the world is the
pitter-patter of little feet—going home.

—Author Unknown

THE BLESSING OF THE FAMILY

Civilization varies with the family, and the family with civilization. Its highest and most complete realization is found where enlightened Christianity prevails; where woman is exalted to her true and lofty place as equal with the man; where husband and wife are one in honor, influence, and affection, and where children are a common bond of care and love. This is the idea of a perfect family.

—William Aikman

_____

How very good and pleasant it is when kindred live together in unity! ... For there the LORD ordained his blessing, life forevermore.

PSALM 133:1, 3 NRSV

*In every conceivable manner, the family is the
link to our past, the bridge to our future.*

—Alex Haley

———————

There is just one way to bring up a child in the
way he should go and that is to travel that way
yourself.

—Abraham Lincoln

———————

A faithful family unit honors God.

An Evening Family Prayer

Lord, behold our family here assembled.
   We thank you for this place in which we dwell,
       for the love that unites us,
   for the peace accorded to us this day,
       for the hope with which we expect the morrow;
   for the health, the work, the food, and the bright skies
       that make our lives delightful;
   for our friends in all parts of the earth. Amen.

   —Robert Louis Stevenson

A farmer who had a quarrelsome family called his sons and told them to lay a bunch of sticks before him. Then, after laying the sticks parallel to one another and binding them, he challenged his sons, one after one, to pick up the bundle and break it. They all tried, but in vain. Then, untying the bundle, he gave them the sticks to break one by one. This they did with the greatest ease. Then said the father, "Thus, my sons, as long as you remain united, you are a match for anything, but differ and separate, and you are undone."

—Aesop

FAMILIES

The linking of generations, the historical lineage of family, the sharing of love ... give purpose to life.

—George Landberg

———————

Some families are big.
Some families are small;
But I love my family best of all!

———————

In our family an experience was not yet finished,
not truly experienced, unless written down and
shared with another.

—Anne Morrow Lindbergh

Dancing with the Father

As a small child perhaps you had the wonderful opportunity to dance with your father. Little feet in white socks frilled with lace moved without effort. Tiny hands grasped in his. Delicate, dainty feet rested securely atop Father's heavy leather work boots—one tiny foot planted firmly on top of his large sturdy shoes.

Now imagine dancing with your heavenly Father. He knows the tune you dance to and the steps required to gracefully complete the waltz of life. Every movement is choreographed within his rhythm—his plan.

Together you flow easily across life's dance floor, never missing a beat as long as you're planted firmly upon him, your hands grasped in his.

But step off or let go of his hands, venturing out on your own, and things quickly become shaky. Suddenly you become aware of the obstacles cluttering the dance floor and realize the imperfections in the floor he so smoothly danced across. You look up as he calls your name … and once again you're secure … dancing with the Father again.

God calls each generation to pass down spiritual truth to the next.

—Dennis Rainey

Children must be valued as our most priceless possession.

—Author Unknown

An effective father devotes himself to become an instrument and model of human experience to his children ... accepts and affirms his children for who they are, appreciates them for what they are accomplishing, and covers them with affection because they are his.

—Gordon MacDonald

Getting to Heaven on Grandma's Apron String

On lazy summer afternoons Susie and her cousin Trish would sit at the kitchen table and talk to Grandma. She would tell them stories from the Bible in response to their abundant questions. Summer after summer they never grew tired of listening to her stories and hearing her talk about heaven as she baked apple turnovers or cooked dinner.

The strings of Grandma's apron often came undone and the girls helped her retie them over and over.

She encouraged the girls to think and talk about God and they all joked that if the heavenly trumpet sounded right then, they could each grab onto an apron string and follow Grandma up to heaven much like a balloon filled with helium disappears into the sky.

Grandma didn't wait for the second coming—she's in heaven now—but both girls know that they'll see Grandma in heaven … and she'll certainly have her apron strings untied.

Grandmas are just antique little girls.

—Author Unknown

There is no greater joy than to know that my children walk with the Lord.

The steps of a good man are ordered by the LORD, And He delights in his way.

PSALM 37:23 NKJV

M ommy, come and lick the cake bowl with me," Molly called.

"Here I come," Mommy said, as she slid around the counter and plunked down next to her daughter, sticking her finger in the bowl.

Don't forget to take time for the little things that come your way—the simple everyday joys of life.

He will yet fill your mouth with laughter and your lips with shouts of joy.

JOB 8:21

THE BLESSING OF REST

Renewal and restoration are not luxuries. Rather, they are essentials. Taking the time to rest and relax for a while is not selfish. Many passages in the Bible emphasize the importance of rest and rejuvenation. Scheduling regular periods of time to relax each week and rewarding yourself with a relaxing, refreshing vacation is as much a spiritual necessity as it is a physical one. Neither you nor your family will benefit if you allow your body and spirit to wear down from a lack of rest. The continual burden of an ultra-busy schedule is not necessarily the mark of a productive life, and over the long term, it can be very harmful to you and those you love.

Jesus knows we must come apart and rest awhile, or else we may just plain come apart.

—Author Unknown

"Come to me and I will give you rest—all of you who work so hard beneath a heavy yoke. Wear my yoke—for it fits perfectly—and let me teach you; for I am gentle and humble, and you shall find rest for your souls; for I give you only light burdens."

MATTHEW 11:28–29 TLB

All work and no rest takes the spring and bound out of the most vigorous life.

—Author Unknown

_____

There are pauses amidst study, and even pauses of seeming idleness, in which a process goes on which may be likened to the digestion of food. In those seasons of repose, the powers are gathering their strength for new efforts; as land which lies fallow recovers itself for tillage.

—J. W. Alexander

_____

Time spent in judicious resting is not time wasted, but time gained.

—Author Unknown

_____

By the seventh day God had finished the work he had been doing; so on the seventh day he rested from all his work. And God blessed the seventh day and made it holy, because on it he rested from all the work of creating that he had done.

GENESIS 2:2–3

Family traditions are blessings that make each family unique and provide us with some of our fondest memories. Perhaps the traditions you now enjoy have been adopted from your and your beloved's childhoods. Likely you have come up with a few that are unique to your present family. Whatever the case, instead of merely going through the motions, purpose to recognize and enjoy the blessing of your family's traditions and use them to bless one another.[5]

You have been my hope, O Sovereign LORD, my confidence since my youth.

PSALM 71:5

Take time to pray as a family. Keep hope alive in your family with all you say and do—at work, rest, and play—through open communication with God.

A Hospitable
HEART

*Do not be interested only in your own life, but be
interested in the lives of others.*

PHILIPPIANS 2:4 NCV

When there is room in the heart, there is room in the house.

—Danish Proverb

———————

In everyone's life, at some time, our inner fire goes out. It is then burst into flame by an encounter with another human being. We should all be thankful for those people who rekindle the inner spirit.

—Albert Schweitzer

———————

May your home always be too small to hold all your friends.

—Irish Blessing

———————

Do something every day to make others happy, even if it's only to leave them alone.

—Author Unknown

AN OPEN HOME

One day Elisha passed through Shunem. A leading lady
of the town talked him into stopping for a meal. And
then it became his custom: Whenever he passed
through, he stopped by for a meal. "I'm certain," said
the woman to her husband, "that this man who stops
by with us all the time is a holy man of God. Why don't
we add on a small room upstairs and furnish it with a
bed and desk, chair and lamp, so that when he comes
by he can stay with us?"

2 KINGS 4:8-17 MSG

Hospitality offers opportunities to cross cultural divides
and break social boundaries.

—Author Unknown

God doesn't forget names—they're written in
permanent ink on his heart.

—Author Unknown

Those who bring sunshine to the lives of others cannot
keep it from themselves.

—Sir James Barrie

A little consideration, a little thought for others,
makes all the difference.

—A. A. Milne

A gossip is one who talks to you about other people.
A bore is one who talks to you about himself.
And a brilliant conversationalist is one who talks
to you about yourself.[6]

—William King

Encouragement is oxygen to the soul.

—George Adams

The crown of the house is
godliness,
The beauty of the house is
order;
The glory of the house is
hospitality,
The blessing of the house
is contentment.

—Henry Van Dyke

Weave a tapestry of compassion.
Make my life a place of warmth
and joy for the people
who pass through it.

A *Model Millionaire*, an 1891 short story by Oscar Wilde, tells a story of Hughie, a young man who stops to visit an artist friend. For a moment he is left alone with the subject of the artist's painting, an old man with the appearance of a vagrant. Hughie gives the beggar a gold coin, which is his spending money for the month. Hughie is moved by the older man, believing he needed the money much more than Hughie did. The beggar smiles, pockets the coin, and thanks Hughie. The reader later finds the beggar is really Baron Hausberg, a millionaire who enjoys modeling for the artist. The Baron sends a wedding gift of ten thousand pounds to Hughie, thanking him for his compassion to help others less fortunate.

Charity is the scope of all God's commands.

—St. Francis of Assisi

THE BLESSING OF GENEROSITY

If you find that life is flat,
Full of this, with none of that,
Try giving!
Introspection makes it flatter;
A few more years—what will it matter?
Try giving!
If the world is dark and bitter;
Things all tend to make a quitter—
Try giving!
Forget yourself in helping others;
Know that all men are your brothers,
You will see then life is sweeter
Than you thought, and far completer—
When you give!

"If you give, you will receive. Your gift will return to you in full measure, pressed down, shaken together to make room for more, and running over."

LUKE 6:38 NLT

Pleasant words are a honeycomb,
sweet to the soul and healing to the bones.

PROVERBS 16:24

———————

Kind words can be short and easy to speak, but their echoes are truly endless.

—Mother Teresa

———————

Kindness is the sunshine in which virtue grows.

—R. G. Ingersoll

———————

Special times together make the most memorable moments in life.

The Beatitudes

Jesus began to teach them, saying: "Blessed are the poor in spirit, for theirs is the kingdom of heaven. Blessed are those who mourn, for they will be comforted. Blessed are the meek, for they will inherit the earth. Blessed are those who hunger and thirst for righteousness, for they will be filled. Blessed are the merciful, for they will be shown mercy. Blessed are the pure in heart, for they will see God.

Blessed are the peacemakers, for they will be called sons of God. Blessed are those who are persecuted because of righteousness, for theirs is the kingdom of heaven. Blessed are you when people insult you, persecute you and falsely say all kinds of evil against you because of me. Rejoice and be glad, because great is your reward in heaven, for in the same way they persecuted the prophets who were before you."

MATTHEW 5:2-12

HOSPITALITY . . .

gives others space to be themselves

offers an atmosphere to relax from the stress of
daily life

welcomes guests with joy

makes a pallet with a pillow or offers a comfort-
able bed

serves a good meal

tells stories that bring laughter

speaks from a generous heart

A hospitable heart makes room for another's story.

—Author Unknown

---

*Now while they were on their way, it occurred
that Jesus entered a certain village, and a
woman named Martha received and welcomed
Him into her house.*

LUKE 10:38 AB

Practice hospitality to one another (those of the household of faith). [Be hospitable, be a lover of strangers, with brotherly affection for the unknown guests, the foreigners, the poor, and all others who come your way who are of Christ's body.] And [in each instance] do it ungrudgingly (cordially and graciously, without complaining but as representing Him).

1 PETER 4:9 AB

LEND A HAND

I am only one,
But still, I am one.
I cannot do everything,
But still, I can do something
And because I cannot do everything
I will not refuse to do something
That I can do.

—Edward Everett Hale

*Volunteers are the only human beings on the face of the earth
who reflect this nation's compassion, unselfish caring,
patience, and just plain loving one another.*

—Erma Bombeck

One great, strong, unselfish soul in every community
could actually redeem the world.

—Elbert Hubbard

*The highest form of worship is the worship of
unselfish Christian service. The greatest form of
praise is the sound of consecrated feet seeking
out the lost and helpless.*

—Billy Graham

*The electricity went out and everything was
dark. Then I heard the strike of a match. The life
of a match lit a candle and comfort and peace
replaced fear from the storm.*

———————

There is no greater joy than to help others see themselves in a positive light.

—Author Unknown

———————

*You are the light of the world.
A city on a hill cannot be hidden.*

MATTHEW 5:14

HOME, SWEET HOME

Mid pleasures and palaces though we may roam,
Be it ever so humble, there's no place like home;
A charm from the sky seems to hallow us there,
Which, seek through the world, is ne'er met with elsewhere.
Home, home, sweet, sweet home!
There's no place like home, oh, there's no place like home!

An exile from home, splendor dazzles in vain;
Oh, give me my lowly thatched cottage again!
The birds singing gayly, that come at my call—
Give me them—and the peace of mind, dearer than all!
Home, home, sweet, sweet home!
There's no place like home, oh, there's no place like home!

I gaze on the moon as I tread the drear wild,
And feel that my mother now thinks of her child,
As she looks on that moon from our own cottage door
Thro' the woodbine, whose fragrance shall cheer me no
    more.
Home, home, sweet, sweet home!
There's no place like home, oh, there's
    no place like home!

How sweet 'tis to sit 'neath a fond father's smile,

And the caress of a mother to soothe and beguile!

Let others delight mid new pleasures to roam,

But give me, oh, give me, the pleasures of home.

Home, home, sweet, sweet home!

There's no place like home, oh, there's no place like home!

To thee I'll return, overburdened with care;

The heart's dearest solace will smile on me there;

No more from that cottage again will I roam;

Be it ever so humble, there's no place like home.

Home, home, sweet, sweet, home!

There's no place like home, oh, there's no place like home!

—John Howard Payne

Among those whom I like or admire, I can find no common denominator, but among those whom I love, I can: all of them make me laugh.

—W. H. Auden

_____

True belly laughter is nothing
but heartfelt prayer.

_____

There is a time for everything, and a season for every activity under heaven: ... a time to laugh ... a time to dance ... a time to embrace.

<small>ECCLESIASTES 3:1, 4–5</small>

_____

Laughing so hard you cry whale tears, fills the bucket of your soul.

Surround yourself with funny people.

———————

IF YOU'RE HAPPY AND YOU KNOW IT!

If you're happy and you know it, clap your hands.
If you're happy and you know it, clap your hands.
If you're happy and you know it, then your face will
*   surely show it.*
If you're happy and you know it, clap your hands.

———————

Laughter smoothes out the
wrinkles in life.

*There never was any heart truly great and gener-
ous that was not also tender and compassionate.*

—Robert Frost

———————

Through the LORD's mercies we are not consumed,
because His compassions fail not. They are new every
morning; great is Your faithfulness. "The LORD is my
portion," says my soul, "Therefore, I hope in Him!"

LAMENTATIONS 3:22–24 NKJV

———————

*The right response can take the most painful
memory and make it a blessing. The wrong
response can end up being very destructive.*

—Charles Stanley

A Warm Reception

Though her husband, Michael, had assured her it would be okay, Patty had been worried about moving to a new neighborhood. Her girls, Rachel and Sarah, were a little shy and in the past had been slow to make new friends. But Patty saw the moving truck pulling up and forgot her concerns in the rush of giving direction as the crew began to unpack their belongings.

The girls were busy rediscovering toys that had been packed away as boxes were delivered to their bedrooms. Gradually Patty became aware that Michael was talking to someone.

"Well, the girls seem to be getting along great," Michael said.

"I've been asking God to send the girls some young friends since we've had a couple families move out of the neighborhood," replied the other man.

Patty walked down the hall toward Rachel's room. Peeking in, she saw three little girls playing with Rachel and Sarah, their collection of Barbies spread across the floor.

Seeing her standing there, Michael called her into the living room. "Hey, honey! This is Pete. He's a single dad and those are his girls playing with Rachel and Sarah."

"It's such a pleasure to meet you, Pete." Patty shook his extended hand warmly. "We were so anxious about the girls making friends here, but it appears that won't be a problem."

"Pete was just saying that there's another family with girls three doors down," said Michael with a smile.

Pete again welcomed them to the neighborhood, called his girls, and prepared to leave. "We'll see you soon, I hope. Let's get together as soon as you're settled."

Patty looked at Michael as soon as he'd gone. "Yes, I believe this is exactly where we're supposed to be."

Michael nodded in agreement.

A heart that welcomes others brings life and friendship to the neighborhood.

When we refrain from giving, with a scarcity mentality, the little we have will become less. When we give generously, with an abundance mentality, what we give away will multiply.

—Henri Nouwen

Give with no strings attached!

The greatest compliment that was ever paid me was when someone asked me what I thought, and attended to my answer.

—Henry David Thoreau

When you remember someone's name, it is like ringing the church bell of their soul.

The soul of man is of the greatest value to God. He gave it the highest price when he gave his only son for a chance that man would want to have a relationship with him.

This is how much God loved the world: He gave his Son, his one and only Son. And this is why: so that no one need be destroyed; by believing in him, anyone can have a whole and lasting life.

John 3:16 msg

FRIENDSHIP
A Gift from God

*Two are better than one, because they have a
good return for their work: If one falls down, his
friend can help him up.*

ECCLESIASTES 4:9–10

Friendship is like a garden. It thrives under little daily attentions: a weed pulled here, the earth loosened there. Do you have friends you value? Send a card today telling them so. If their lives are a blessing to you, turn around and bless them by letting them know.

One may have a blazing hearth in one's soul and yet no one ever came to sit by it. Passers-by see only a wisp of smoke from the chimney and continue on their way.

—Vincent van Gogh

When we honestly ask ourselves which person in our lives means the most to us, we often find that it is those who, instead of giving advice, solutions, or cures, have chosen rather to share our pain and touch our wounds with a warm and tender hand.

—Henri Nouwen

A HOME SONG

I read within a poet's book
A word that starred the page:
"Stone walls do not a prison make,
Nor iron bars a cage!"

Yes, that is true; and something more
You'll find, where'er you roam,
That marble floors and gilded walls
Can never make a home.

But every house where Love abides,
And Friendship is a guest,
Is surely home, and home-sweet-home:
For there the heart can rest.[7]

—Henry van Dyke

*I had three chairs in my house; one for soli-
tude, two for friendship, three for society.*

—Henry David Thoreau

A day without a friend is like a pot without a single drop of honey left inside.

—A. A. Milne, author of *Winnie-the-Pooh*

_____

Good friends are hard to find, difficult to leave, and impossible to forget.

—Author Unknown

_____

Friends are family you find along the way.

—Author Unknown

_____

A true friend is one who comes in when the whole world goes out.

—Author Unknown

An Extra Set of Hands

Marta dipped the last strawberry into the melted chocolate and placed it on the platter to harden. It was taking her longer than she had expected to prepare for the wedding shower tomorrow. As she placed the empty bowl in the sink, she caught a glimpse of her neighbor Jan's house. She realized she hadn't seen the young mother of four for a couple of days. They often saw each other at the mailbox or waved hello when Jan took the kids to the park each afternoon.

I hope she's doing okay, Marta thought. I should go check on her, but I've got so much to do. As Marta headed downstairs to put a load of towels in the washing machine, she couldn't let go of her concern for her friend. She shut the washing machine lid and decided to follow her instinct and check in on Jan.

When she reached the front porch of Jan's house, she saw that it was dark inside the house. She rang the doorbell and a couple of minutes later four-year-old Tandy pulled back the side window curtains. A few minutes later Jan opened the door still in her pajamas, obviously sick and holding a fussy baby Emily.

"Jan, you look terrible. Why didn't you call me?" asked Marta anxiously.

"I knew you had to get ready for the bridal shower—" Jan began.

"Nonsense. You should have called me," said Marta, as she took the baby from Jan. "Tandy, go get your Barbies and we'll play while Mommy takes a nap." Tandy hurried to her room while Marta urged Jan back to her room and to bed.

"Jan, you get some rest. I'll take care of the kids for a few hours and get the twins started on their homework when they get home from school," said Marta. She closed the bedroom door and cooed soothingly to Emily as she retreated down the hall to the family room, where Tandy had already begun to unpack her Barbie case.

A friend offers a second set of hands when you need four hands instead of two.

A true friend is always loyal, and a brother is born to help in time of need.

PROVERBS 17:17 TLB

———————

A friend is one who knows you as you are, understands where you've been, accepts who you've become, and still gently invites you to grow.

———————

I wonder what Piglet is doing, thought Pooh. I wish I were there to be doing it, too.

—A. A. Milne, *Winnie-the-Pooh*

A PRAYER OF BLESSING FOR A FRIEND

May God bless you, my wonderful friend! May you know how special you are to me and how thankful I am for your friendship. May the joy you bring to others be returned to you many times over, and may you experience life in all its fullness.

May your relationships be rich and meaningful, and may you never know loneliness. May God comfort you in times of sadness and grief, so sorrow cannot overtake you. May you be kept from all harm and be blessed with good health. May your life be a long one, surpassing your expectations.

May you never know lack but have all your needs met. Instead of being seized by fear during difficult times, may you take refuge next to God's heart. May you be wise in your decisions and discerning in all your ways. May you experience success in everything you do.

Most of all may you realize how precious you are to God. He loves you so much that he continually thinks of you, and I believe you bring a smile to his face. Regardless of the challenges you face, may he work everything out for your good and give you peace.

Amen.

After the friendship of God, a friend's affection is the greatest treasure here below.

—Author Unknown

God and man exist for each other and neither is satisfied without the other.

—Author Unknown

We pursue God because, and only because, he has first put an urge within us that spurs us to the pursuit.

—A. W. Tozer

It is God's will that we believe that we see him continually, though it seems to us that the sight be only partial; and through this belief he makes us always to gain more grace. For God wishes to be seen, and he wishes to be sought, and he wishes to be expected, and he wishes to be trusted.

—Julian of Norwich

TIME WITH GOD

R ay tapped his brakes a little harder than he had meant to. Traffic was heavy but the driver behind him seemed to be paying attention. Tammy and the kids were out of town for another week so he was headed home to a quiet, dark house. He smiled a little at the thought of the fanfare he normally received when he opened the front door.

Anna, Jacob, and Holly would squeal with delight and cries of "Daddy's home!" echoed through the house. Ray always had to drop his briefcase—and anything else in his hands—in order to gather them all into his arms. His heart warmed at the thought.

Just as they anticipate your homecoming, I anticipate your time with me. Ray felt the Lord speaking to his heart. There was no need to be depressed because of his family's absence. Someone special was waiting for him. And Ray knew he could embrace God's presence without even getting out of the car.

Look! I have been standing at the door and I am constantly knocking. If anyone hears me calling him and opens the door, I will come in and fellowship with him and he with me.

REVELATION 3:20 TLB

Good friends make good times even better.

—Author Unknown

Friendships are possible only when we open the window of our heart and allow the sunshine of someone's life to come in.

—Ginny Hobson and Sherry Morris

A true friend warms you with her presence, trusts you with her secrets, and remembers you in her prayers.

—Author Unknown

Faithful are the wounds of a friend, but the kisses of an enemy are deceitful.

PROVERBS 27:6 KJV

*Forgiveness is a funny thing—it warms the heart
and cools the sting.*

—Marlene Dietrich

———————

*When you forgive, you in no way change the past—
but you sure do change the future.*

—Bernard Meltzer

———————

I can forgive, but I cannot forget, is only another way of
saying I will not forgive. Forgiveness ought to be like a
cancelled note—torn in two, and burned up, so that it
never can be shown against one.

—Henry Ward Beecher

THE BRIDGE BUILDER

An old man, going a lone highway,
Came at the evening, cold and gray,
To a chasm, vast and deep and wide,
Through which was flowing a sullen tide.
The old man crossed in the twilight dim;
The sullen stream had no fears for him;
But he turned when safe on the other side
And built a bridge to span the tide.

"Old man," said a fellow pilgrim near,
"You are wasting strength with building here;
Your journey will end with the ending day;
You never again must pass this way;
You have crossed the chasm, deep and wide
Why build you the bridge at the eventide?"

The builder lifted his old gray head:

"Good friend, in the path I have come," he said,

"There followeth after me today

A youth whose feet must pass this way.

This chasm that has been naught to me

To that fair-haired youth may a pitfall be.

He, too, must cross in the twilight dim;

Good friend, I am building the bridge for him."

—Will Allen Dromgoole

When friends gather, hearts warm.

—Author Unknown

If I could search for one true friend
and seek until the very end,
I'd find out what I always knew:
there is no better friend than you!

—Roy Lessin

The best antiques are old friends.

—Author Unknown

PRAY FOR ME

Here is where the road divides.
Here is where we realize
The sculpting of the Father's great design.
Through time you've been a friend to me
But time is now the enemy.
I wish we didn't have to say goodbye,
But I know the road he chose for me
Is not the road he chose for you,
So as we chase the dreams we're after

Pray for me and I'll pray for you,
Pray that we will keep the common ground.
Won't you pray for me and I'll pray for you
And one day love will bring us back around.

—Michael W. Smith

Of all the music that reached farthest into heaven, it is the beating of a loving heart.

—Henry Ward Beecher

———————

Friendship isn't a big thing—it's a million little things.

—Author Unknown

———————

Don't walk in front of me, I may not follow.
Don't walk behind me, I may not lead.
Just walk beside me and be my friend.

—Albert Camus

Do not forsake your friend and the friend of your father.

PROVERBS 27:10

THE MIRACLE OF FRIENDSHIP

There is a miracle called friendship
That dwells within the heart.
You don't know how it happens
Or when it gets its start.
But the happiness it brings you
Always gives you a special life
And you realize that friendship
Is God's most precious gift.

—Author Unknown

Friendship doubles our joy and divides our grief.

—Swedish Proverb

True friendship will weather the
storm of life with you.

—Author Unknown

———————

We are friends for life.

When we are together the years fall away.

Isn't that what matters?

To have someone who can remember with you?

To have someone who remembers how far you've come?

—Judy Blume

———————

A true friend holds your heart together while it's breaking and stands strong, helping you put the pieces back together.

—Author Unknown

Friendship is reaching for someone's hand and touching their heart.

—Author Unknown

_____

My friend, you are in my heart,
whether near or far apart.

—Author Unknown

_____

Friendship is like a patchwork quilt of caring words, thoughtful deeds, and lots of laughter, all stitched together with understanding.

—Author Unknown

_____

Dear friend, I am praying that all is well
with you and that your body is as
healthy as I know your soul is.

3 JOHN 2 NLT

Warming the Hearts
of Your
NEIGHBORS

*You shall love your neighbor as yourself. There is
no other commandment greater than these.*

MARK 12:31 NKJV

All things grow with love.

The most beautiful things in the world
cannot be seen or even touched, they must
be felt with the heart.

—Helen Keller

A good neighbor is a welcomed blessing.

—Author Unknown

How can I say thanks for the things you
have done for me? Things so undeserved,
yet you gave to prove your love to me. The
voices of a million angels could not express
my gratitude. All that I am and ever hope
to be, I owe it all to thee.

—Andrae Crouch

ACROSS THE STREET

Darin stepped outside and carefully made his way across the icy sidewalk in front of his home to retrieve the mail. The weatherman had predicted six inches of snow, but it had come in the form of an ice storm instead. Days had passed and few had ventured out of their homes except to put salt on their sidewalks.

He glanced across the street toward his elderly neighbor's home. *I wonder how Earl and Henny are doing, he thought. Maybe I should check to see if they need something from the grocery store.* He half skated, half walked across the road, stopping at their mailbox to collect the stack of mail, and maneuvered his way onto the front porch.

Eighty-five-year-old Henny was waiting for him and opened the front door to greet him. "Come in, come in," she said. "How 'bout this storm?"

"Yep, it was a doozy! Didn't want you trying to get to your mailbox in this mess," Darin replied with a grin. "I thought I'd bring it to you."

Henny thanked him profusely and they chatted for a few minutes more about the storm and what the weatherman was predicting for the weekend.

"I'm going to venture out to the grocery store this afternoon. Do you need anything?"

"Oh, no," she said, "the boys have both been by with groceries so we're all set. Thanks for thinking of us, though." She gave Darin a quick hug and reached forward to open the door. "You be careful out there," she urged as she ushered him out.

As Darin skated his way back home he felt a warm glow inside. His neighbors knew that he cared enough to check in on them. In his heart he resolved to do it more often … not just when they had bad weather.

Believe in yourself, your neighbors, your work, your ultimate attainment of more complete happiness. It is only the farmer who faithfully plants seeds in the spring, who reaps a harvest in autumn.

—B. C. Forbes

_____

Little deeds of kindness, little words of love, help to make earth happy like the heaven above.

—Julia Carney

_____

God is a fire that warms and kindles the heart and inward parts.... He will come to warm our hearts with perfect love, not only for him but also for our neighbor....

—St. Seraphim of Sarov

*It is not that I want merely to be called a
Christian, but actually to be one. Yes, if I prove to
be one, then I can have the name.*

—Ignatius of Antioch

———————

A four-year-old child's next-door neighbor, an elderly
gentleman, had recently lost his wife. When the little
boy saw the man crying, he went into the gentleman's
yard, climbed onto his lap, and sat there for quite some
time. When his mother asked what he had been doing
while at the neighbor's house, the little boy said,
"Nothing. I just helped him cry."

———————

*The LORD has chosen and sent me to tell the oppressed
the good news, to heal the brokenhearted, and to
announce freedom for prisoners and captives. This is
the year when the LORD God will show kindness to us
and punish our enemies. The LORD has sent me to
comfort those who mourn, especially in Jerusalem. He
sent me to give them flowers in place of their sorrow,
olive oil in place of tears, and joyous praise in place of
broken hearts. They will be called "Trees of Justice,"
planted by the LORD to honor his name.*

ISAIAH 61:1-3 CEV

There is no better exercise for your heart than reaching down and helping to lift someone up.

—Bernard Meltzer

Sometimes just a smile on our face,
   Can help to make this world a better place.
Stand up for the things that are right.
   Try to talk things out instead of fight.
Lend a hand when you can, get involved, this is good.
   You can help to make a difference in your
      neighborhood.

—Robert Alan

Live as if everything you do will eventually be known.

—Hugh Prather

There are nine requisites for contented living:

HEALTH enough to make work a pleasure;

WEALTH enough to support your needs;

STRENGTH enough to battle with difficulties and
    forsake them;

GRACE enough to confess your sins and overcome
    them;

PATIENCE enough to toil until some good is
    accomplished;

CHARITY enough to see some good in your neighbor;

LOVE enough to move you to be useful and helpful to
    others;

FAITH enough to make real the things of God;

HOPE enough to remove all anxious fears concerning
    the future.

—Johann Wolfgang von Goethe

---

*Each of us should please his neighbor for his
good, to build him up.*

ROMANS 15:2

The friend who can be silent with us in a moment of despair or confusion, who can stay with us in an hour of grief and bereavement, who can tolerate not knowing, not curing, not healing, and face with us the reality of our powerlessness, that is a friend who cares.

—Henri Nouwen

Jesus answered: "Love the Lord your God with all your heart and with all your soul and with all your strength and with all your mind and, Love your neighbor as yourself."

LUKE 10:27

Certain thoughts are prayers. There are moments when, whatever be the attitude of the body, the soul is on its knees.

—Victor Hugo

———————

Let God's promises shine on your problems.

—Corrie ten Boom

———————

"What do you think of God," the teacher asked. After a pause, the young pupil replied, "He's not a think, he's a feel."

—Paul Frost

Perhaps one of the most loving and yet most difficult things we can do is pray for our neighbors.

PRAYER FOR MY NEIGHBORS

Lord, thank you for my neighbors
Up and down the street.
I ask you to give them understanding
When my yard is not so neat.

Help me to show them your love
Through the things I do and say.
And give them many opportunities
To see your love in me each day.

Help me to hold my tongue
When they're angry and complain.
And give me words of encouragement for them
When I know they've had a bad day.

I pray those who are lonely
Will find comfort with friendship.
I pray you'll bring prosperity
To their hearts and souls.
I pray that you'll help them find their destiny
In you along the way.

Lord, bless my many neighbors
Up and down the street.
Give me the courage to introduce you
To every one of them I greet.

———————

*I stand at the door and knock; if anyone hears
and listens to and heeds My voice and opens the
door, I will come in to him and will eat with him,
and he [will eat] with Me.*

A heart filled with love always has something to give.

—Author Unknown

It is, in fact, Christian love which discovers and knows that one's neighbor exists and that ... it is one and the same thing ... everyone is one's neighbor. If it were not a duty to love, then, there would be no concept of neighbor at all. But only when one loves his neighbor, only then is the selfishness of preferential love rooted out and the equality of the eternal preserved.

—Søren Kierkegaard

After the verb "to love," the verb, "to help" is the most beautiful verb in the world.

—Bertha Von Suttner

The love of our neighbor in all its fullness simply means being able to say to him, "What are you going through?"

—Simone Weil

Those that we work with eight hours a day are just as much our neighbors as those who live on our street. To love your neighbor takes faith to look at them through God's eyes. If you work together then you've got to see yourself working with them as a team.

—Author Unknown

The Crayon Box That Talked is a story of a box of crayons. Two colors didn't like each other and weren't getting along. But as each saw the other work his gift of color, they discovered they could create beauty together that they could never attain alone. This book illustrates what we can accomplish when we work together in spite of our differences. By depending on each other's strengths and picking the other up when they fall, we can do more together than on our own.[8]

Together we can grow up, develop our gifts, and express our talents. Together we can discover we are free to become who God created us to be as individuals, within the environment of community. Through simple acts of kindness—words of encouragement, cheer, applause, compassion, and loving correction—your team can touch each other with God's kindness and succeed.

We are a box of crayons, each one of us unique. But when we get together the picture is more complete.

—Shane DeRolf, **The Crayon Box That Talked**

The good neighbor looks beyond the external accidents and discerns those inner qualities that make all men human and, therefore, brothers.

—Martin Luther King, Jr.

———————

Contributing to the success of others could someday prove to be your greatest accomplishment in life.

—Author Unknown

———————

The best gift you can give is a hug: one size fits all and nobody ever minds if you return it!

—Author Unknown

LOVE EACH OTHER

Let us ever love each other
With a heart that's warm and true,
Ever doing to our brother
As to us we'd have him do.

When the heart is sad and lonely,
And the eyes with tears o'erflow,
Gentle words and deeds of kindness
Fall like sunbeams on the snow.

Let us help our fallen brother,
Lift him gently by the hand;
Speaking words of cheer and comfort,
Point him to a better land.

In this world of toil and sorrow
Many hearts are full of care,
Let us live to serve our Master,
And each other's burdens bear.

Kind and loving to each other,
Gentle words to all we meet;
Thus we follow Christ our Savior,
Proving all his service sweet.

—William J. Henry

*Let us not judge one another anymore, but
rather resolve this, not to put a stumbling block
or a cause to fall in our brother's way.*

ROMANS 14:13 NKJV

———

Admonish thy friends in secret, praise them openly.

—Publilius Syrus

———

*What is extraordinary, exceptional,
and breathtaking about another person?
Shout it to the world!*

—Author Unknown

When God prompts you to do something, do it!

—Author Unknown

---

*Too often we underestimate the power
of a touch, a smile, a kind word, a listening ear,
an honest compliment, or the smallest act of
caring, all of which have the potential
to turn a life around.*

—Leo Buscaglia

---

*A lost soul can always find
hope in a friend.*

—Author Unknown

Words that mean a lot:

 I'm here for you.

 I love you.

 I miss you.

 I'll listen.

And sometimes you don't have to say anything. Your presence, your listening ear, a phone call when times are hard says it all.

———————

How sweet and gracious, even in common speech,
Is that fine sense which men call Courtesy!
Wholesome as air and genial as the light,
Welcome in every clime as breath of flowers,
It transmutes aliens into trusting friends,
And gives its owner passport round the globe.

     —James Thomas Fields

Surely you heard of him and were taught in him in accordance with the truth that is in Jesus. You were taught, with regard to your former way of life, to put off your old self, which is being corrupted by its deceitful desires; to be made new in the attitude of your minds; and to put on the new self, created to be like God in true righteousness and holiness. Therefore each of you must put off falsehood and speak truthfully to his neighbor, for we are all members of one body.

EPHESIANS 4:21–25

———————

No one is rich enough to do without a neighbor.

—Danish Proverb

———————

May the road rise to meet you,
May the wind always be at your back,
May the sunshine warm your face,
The rains fall upon your fields and,
Until we meet again,
May God hold you in the palm of his hand.

—Irish Blessing

LOVE
Is a Verb

Let all that you do be done with love.

Our love is what draws others to God. Everywhere we go and in everything we do, we leave evidence of our presence in the lives of others. It is God's hope that we leave an impression of his love on the hearts of others.

———————

Love is life. All, everything that I understand, I understand only because I love. Everything is, everything exists, only because I love. Everything is united by it alone. Love is God, and to die means that I, a particle of love, shall return to the general and eternal source.

—Leo Tolstoy

———————

If the person you are talking to doesn't appear to be listening, be patient. It may simply be that he has a small piece of fluff in his ear.

—A. A. Milne

LOVE ENCOURAGES.

Love is a cheerleader for your soul! With a "can do" spirit, love continues to believe you can—even when you're four touchdowns behind.

————

Treat people as if they were what they ought to be and you help them to become what they are capable of being.

—Johann Wolfgang von Goethe

————

All of the beautiful sentiments in the world weigh less than a single lovely action.

—James Russell Lowell

LOVE BY FAITH

There are many beautiful love stories in the Bible. One of them is the story of Isaac and Rebekah in Genesis 24 and it begins with a blind date. As you read the story in Genesis you will find that Rebecca didn't meet Isaac until she had accepted his engagement. Talk about a blind date. She obeyed God, left her family, and traveled with Abraham's servant back to Isaac's homeland to meet and marry him. Rebekah loved by faith.

———

May the Lord make your love to grow and over-flow to each other and to everyone else, just as our love does toward you. This will result in your hearts being made strong, sinless and holy by God our Father, so that you may stand before him guiltless on that day when our Lord Jesus Christ returns with all those who belong to him.

1 THESSALONIANS 3:12–13 TLB

Circumstances never create character; they merely reveal it.

—John Blanchard

———————

Love throws fear overboard. Fear wants to separate us from God's best, but love calls to us in faith and we are no longer afraid. Fear loses its influence at the sound of love's voice and faith carries us past fear to a confident place in God.

———————

Love's motivator is to draw attention to God and those around you.

LOVE BELIEVES

Love believes the Bible, God's Word, and is fully persuaded that what God says he will do. Love believes for God's best and focuses on: "whatsoever things are true, whatsoever things are honest, whatsoever things are just, whatsoever things are pure, whatsoever things are lovely, whatsoever things are of good report; if there be any virtue, and if there be any praise, [love] think[s] on these things."

PHILIPPIANS 4:8 KJV

Love lives a life rich in mercy.

—Author Unknown

Love is sharing your popcorn.

—Charles Schulz

At the heart of mankind's existence is the desire to be intimate and to be loved by another.

—Gary Chapman

Love Covers

Till I loved I never lived—enough.

—Emily Dickinson

I am convinced that nothing can ever separate us from his love. Death can't, and life can't. The angels won't, and all the powers of hell itself cannot keep God's love away.

Romans 8:38 TLB

Tattletales expose the flaws and mistakes of others, but love covers the sins of those around us.

In his love he clothes us, and enfolds and embraces us; that tender love completely surrounds us, never to leave us. As I saw it he is everything that is good.

—Julian of Norwich

LOVE REJOICES

Love rejoices in the truth; Love discovers joy all over again. When we choose to love no matter what, we can get past all the facts of why we don't want to love and focus on the truth that love is the very point of our creation. Love is our destiny.

Love is to the heart what the summer is to the farmer's year. It brings to harvest all the loveliest flowers of the soul.

—Billy Graham

LOVE SERVES

Picture that person in your life who goes the extra mile. When they see a need, they're immediately taking care of it. If your tea glass is half full—they're filling it. They have an open heart and home, and are eager to bless others wherever and whenever they can.

———————

A rose can say I love you,
Orchids can enthrall,
But a weed bouquet in a chubby fist,
Oh my, that says it all!

—Author Unknown

———————

[Jesus] took the children in his arms, put his hands on them and blessed them.

MARK 10:16

But true love is a durable fire,
In the mind ever burning,
Never sick, never old, never dead,
From itself never turning.

—Sir Walter Raleigh

———————

And we have known and believed the love that
God has for us. God is love, and he who abides
in love abides in God, and God in him.

1 JOHN 4:16 NKJV

———————

God's desire for relationship continues to draw us to
him by love working in us. God pursues us with an
undying passion. Love is his makeup—his essence—his
character.

—Author Unknown

As for that which is beyond your strength, be absolutely certain that our Lord loves you, devotedly and individually, loves you just as you are.... Accustom yourself to the wonderful thought that God loves you with a tenderness, a generosity, and an intimacy that surpasses all your dreams. Give yourself up with joy to a loving confidence in God and have courage to believe firmly that God's action toward you is a masterpiece of partiality and love. Rest tranquilly in this abiding conviction.

—Abbé Henri de Tourville

*The whole worth of a kind deed lies in the love
that inspires it.*

—The Talmud

———————

Love me without fear

Trust me without questioning

Need me without demanding

Want me without restrictions

Accept me without change

Desire me without inhibitions

For a love so free ...

Will never fly away.

—Dick Sutphen

Laughter adds richness, texture, and color to otherwise ordinary days. It is a gift, a choice, a discipline, and an art.

—Tim Hansel

———————

To love a person
Is to learn the song
That is in their heart
And to sing it to them
When they have forgotten it.

—Author Unknown

———————

A psalm of David; the servant of the LORD. He sang this song to the LORD on the day the LORD rescued him from all his enemies and from Saul. I love you, Lord; you are my strength.

PSALM 18:1 NLT

Love doesn't seek out beauty. Love, instead, creates beauty by its affection. There is no more durable beauty in a woman than that created by the enduring love and appreciation which her husband gives her each day, each year, for a lifetime.

_____

For it was not into my ear you whispered,
but into my heart. It was not my lips
you kissed, but my soul.

—Judy Garland

_____

The hunger for love is much more difficult to remove than the hunger for bread.

—Mother Teresa

I pray that Christ will be more and more at home in your hearts, living within you as you trust in him. May your roots go down deep into the soil of God's marvelous love; and may you be able to feel and understand, as all God's children should, how long, how wide, how deep, and how high his love really is; and to experience this love for yourselves, though it is so great that you will never see the end of it or fully know or understand it. And so at last you will be filled up with God himself.

Ephesians 3:17–19 tlb

God loves each of us as if there were only one of us.

—Augustine of Hippo

Unconditional love—a rare and precious gift. But even those who love us most will let us down at some point. It's part of being human, though most have good intentions. There is one who will never disappoint you, however. In fact, God is love. He loves you more than you can fathom, and he will never let you down. In fact, there is nothing you could ever do to change his love for you. Talk about a blessing!

To love abundantly is to live abundantly, and to love forever is to live forever.

—Henry Drummond

I LOVE THEE

I love thee—I love thee!
'Tis all that I can say;
It is my vision in the night,
My dreaming in the day;
The very echo of my heart,
The blessings when I pray:
I love thee—I love thee!
Is all that I can say.

I love thee—I love thee!
Is ever on my tongue;
In all my proudest poesy
That chorus still is sung;
It is the verdict of my eyes,
Amidst the gay and young:
I love thee—I love thee!
A thousand maids among.

I love thee—I love thee!
Thy bright and hazel glance,
The mellow lute upon those lips,
Whose tender tones entrance;
But most, dear heart of hearts, thy proofs
That still these words enhance.
I love thee—I love thee!
Whatever be thy chance.

—Thomas Hood

---

*Love is an act of endless forgiveness, a tender
look which becomes a habit.*

—Peter Ustinov

One pardons to the degree that one loves.

—François de La Rochefoucauld

---

*Bear with each other and forgive whatever griev-
ances you may have against one another. Forgive
as the Lord forgave you.*

COLOSSIANS 3:13

It is love that asks, that seeks, that knocks, that finds, and that is faithful to what it finds.

—Augustine of Hippo

———

Love makes things grow.

—Anonymous

Love Lives Strong

Peter's divorce had been nasty. His wife, Sonya, had gone for the jugular after promising that she'd make sure he never saw the kids. She'd accused him of every vile thing she could imagine—and most of it was untrue.

He struggled to keep his composure while she was on the witness stand lying about his infidelities and mistreatment of her and the children. Peter prayed continually throughout the ordeal. He didn't want to take his kids from their mother, but he needed to remain a permanent part of their lives.

When the court awarded temporary custody to Sonya, Peter felt his heart would explode. It seemed he was no longer breathing, stuck in a body that had turned to stone. His strength and power left him. He thought he would collapse as his attorney guided him out of the courtroom.

Peter sat in his car, trying not to entertain the thoughts that begged entrance to his brain. He could not imagine life without his children. "God, give me strength and power to endure this," he prayed. Even as he finished praying, he felt an infusion of physical and mental energy.

He reached for his Bible, opened it to the Psalms, and began to read the words of David as he encouraged himself in the Lord. As he read, he became confident that God would give him exactly what he'd asked for—the power to take another step and live another day through this crisis.

He has achieved success who has lived well,
laughed often, and loved much.

—Bessie Anderson Stanley

———————

Love doesn't make the world go round. Love is what
makes the ride worthwhile.

—Franklin P. Jones

———————

We can do no great things—only small things with
great love.

—Mother Teresa

Love is water in the desert of life.

—Anonymous

As the deer pants for streams of water, so my soul pants for you, O God. My soul thirsts for God, for the living God. When can I go and meet with God? My tears have been my food day and night, while men say to me all day long, "Where is your God?" These things I remember as I pour out my soul: how I used to go with the multitude, leading the procession to the house of God, with shouts of joy and thanksgiving among the festive throng. Why are you downcast, O my soul? Why so disturbed within me? Put your hope in God, for I will yet praise him, my Savior and my God.... Deep calls to deep in the roar of your waterfalls; all your waves and breakers have swept over me. By day the LORD directs his love, at night his song is with me—a prayer to the God of my life.

PSALM 42:1–8

ACTS OF LOVE:

Affection

Adoration

Worship

Nurture

Protection

Support

Devotion

Discipline

Respect

Admiration

Investment

Cultivation

Cherishing

Encouragement

God's love is so extensive that it covers the whole world, but so minute that he concerns himself with me.

———————

If a man owns a hundred sheep, and one of them wanders away, will he not leave the ninety-nine on the hills and go to look for the one that wandered off?

MATTHEW 18:12

———————

God's grand purpose is to bring every man, woman, and child back into fellowship with him. As the ultimate Father, he doesn't want to be separated from his creation. He loves us more than we could ever comprehend.

———

God so loved the world he gave his one and only son that whoever believes in him shall not perish but have eternal life.

JOHN 3:16

SOURCES

www.bartleby.com
www.great-quotes.com
www.time.com
www.giga-usa.com
www.appleseeds.org
www.compleatmother.com
www.quotegarden.com
www.poetryconnection.net
www.childfun.com
www.myfavoritezines.com
www.beliefnet.com
http://thinkexist.com
http://inspire.luquette.org
www.allgreatquotes.com
www.amazon.com
www.43things.com
www.snopes.com
www.betterworld.net

www.love-poems.me.uk
www.poetry-archive.com
www.k12tlc.org
www.michaelwsmith.com
www.wow4u.com
www.heritagegreetingcards.com
www.scrapbook.com
www.gardendigest.com
www.christianitytoday.com
http://tiawanamama.blogspot.com
www.quotemountain.com
www.quotationspage.com
http://library.timelesstruths.org
http://goodtheology.com
www.brownielocks.com
http://quotes.zaadz.com
www.poemhunter.com

NOTES

1. *Time,* December 5, 1960, http://www.time.com/time/magazine/
   article/0,9171,895060,00.html.

2. Till the Boys Come Home! (Song), 1914,
   http://www.bartleby.com/66/64/22564.html.

3. *Collected Verse of Edgar Guest* (NY: Buccaneer Books, 1976), p. 569,
   http://www.appleseeds.org/home-prayer_guest.htm.

4. "Home Is Where You Are Happy," *Time,* July 8, 1985.

5. *The Book of Blessings for Couples* (Colorado Springs: Honor Books, 2003), p. 54.

6. John C. Maxwell and Les Parrott, *25 Ways to Win with People* (Nashville: Thomas
   Nelson, 2005).

7. "A Home Song" by Henry van Dyke, reprinted from *The White Bees and Other
   Poems* (New York: Scribner & Son, 1909), http://www.poetry-
   archive.com/v/a_home_song.html.

8. Shane DeRolf, *The Crayon Box that Talked* (New York: Random House, 1996).

SCRIPTURE SOURCES

HONOR BOOKS

expressions of faith, hope, and love

*The LORD will send a blessing on your barns and on every-
thing you put your hand to. The LORD your God will bless
you in the land he is giving you.*

DEUTERONOMY 28:8

The fruit of righteousness will be peace; the effect of righteousness will be quietness and confidence forever. My people will live in peaceful dwelling places, in secure homes, in
undisturbed places of rest.

ISAIAH 32:17–18

The LORD'S curse is on the house of the wicked, but he blesses the
home of the righteous.

PROVERBS 3:33

Lord, I believe that you have provided me with the blessing
of a home so that I might be a blessing to others. Give me
wisdom, compassion, and a spirit of hospitality to create an
oasis of peace as I welcome people into my home. I ask
your continued blessing on me and my family and all of the
friends, extended family, and neighbors that we host in our
home. Give me the grace to extend your blessings to all
those I come in contact with and fill me with thanksgiving
as you continue to BLESS THIS HOME! Amen.

BUT THE GREATEST OF THESE IS LOVE!

I f I speak with human eloquence and angelic ecstasy but don't love, I'm nothing but the creaking of a rusty gate. If I speak God's Word with power, revealing all his mysteries and making everything plain as day, and if I have faith that says to a mountain, "Jump," and it jumps, but I don't love, I'm nothing. If I give everything I own to the poor and even go to the stake to be burned as a martyr, but I don't love, I've gotten nowhere. So, no matter what I say, what I believe, and what I do, I'm bankrupt without love. Love never gives up. Love cares more for others than for self. Love doesn't want what it doesn't have. Love doesn't strut, doesn't have a swelled head, doesn't force itself on others, isn't always "me first," doesn't fly off the handle, doesn't keep score of the sins of others, doesn't revel when others grovel, takes pleasure in the flowering of truth, puts up with anything, trusts God always, always looks for the best, never looks back, but keeps going to the end. Love never dies. Inspired speech will be over some day; praying in tongues will end; understanding will reach its limit. We know only a portion of the truth, and what we say about God is always incomplete. But when the Complete arrives, our incompletes will be canceled. When I was an infant at my mother's breast, I gurgled and cooed like any infant. When I grew up, I left those infant ways for good. We don't yet see things clearly. We're squinting in a fog, peering through a mist. But it won't be long before the weather clears and the sun shines bright! We'll see it all then, see it all as clearly as God sees us, knowing him directly just as he knows us! *But for right now, until that completeness, we have three things to do to lead us toward that consummation: Trust steadily in God, hope unswervingly, love extravagantly. And the best of the three is love* (1 Cor. 13:1–13).